DENBIGh

A Pictorial History
Volume 2

DENBIGH

A Pictorial History
Volume 2

by

R.M. Owen

Foreword

by

E.P. Williams

The cover illustration shows the easterly end of Denbigh High Street in 1903 with the
County Hall prominent.

Printed by Gee & Son (Denbigh) Ltd., Chapel Street, Denbigh

CONTENTS

FOREWORD

R.M. Owen, in compiling a second Pictorial History of his beloved Denbigh, has done us all, Denbighites and others alike, a great favour. The first publication has been much enjoyed and treasured and we have waited patiently for four years for its successor.

These pictorial records, now appearing in many towns and districts, may be counted as most valuable contributions to the volumes of local history now increasingly available. They capture for all time a permanent picture of buildings long demolished and a way of life which might otherwise be completely forgotten.

Denbigh has played a very prominent part in the history of Wales and indeed of Britain as a whole. Its importance is reflected in many of the pictures, likewise features of the life of the town, which are not to be found elsewhere.

E.P. Williams

ACKNOWLEDGEMENTS

Mrs Doris Boycott, Mrs Joan Pritchard, Mrs A Oliver Davies, Mrs E Jones, Miss Aldwyth Williams, Mr and Mrs Huw Pritchard, Mr & Mrs Peter Thomas and Mr Humphrey Adams Jones for lending photographs.

Mr E Price Williams for reading the manuscript.

The Archivist and Staff at Ruthin Record Office for their guidance and assistance.

Mr Alun Williams of Gwasg Gee for his advice and cooperation.

INTRODUCTION

In this second presentation of Denbigh through postcards and other pictures, an attempt has been made to cover some of the topics not previously included. Rather than presenting a sequence of scenes in the form of a town trail, as in Volume I, the pictures this time have been grouped according to subject. Inevitably, there is again an emphasis on the Town Centre streets, with Shops and associated activities receiving particular attention. Trade and Industry also feature prominently, as these aspects reflect most accurately the lives of ordinary people.

An important consideration in this type of publication is the need to thoroughly research the background of each picture. This is often best accomplished through conversation with older members of the community, who have a wealth of information about the town and its history. I am accordingly particularly grateful to those of you who have borne the burden of my quest for information with tolerance and courtesy.

It is evident that even with this second volume, we still have, what is at best, only a sketchy representation of Denbigh's pictorial history.

There is already sufficient material available to form the basis of another publication, but this can only be sufficiently comprehensive if that storehouse of hitherto unseen postcards and pictures, held by individuals, is made available. Letters, billheads, deeds and personal manuscripts, including diaries, also contain vital information and there is always the danger that these items are sometimes consigned to the scrapheap. Many thanks are of course due to those of you, too numerous to mention by name, whose contributions have already been of such great significance in my work.

BIBLIOGRAPHY

Historic Denbigh (1983) David Castledine & R M Owen
The Buildings of Wales (Clwyd) (1986) Edward Hubbard
Eminent Men of Denbighshire (1946) H Ellis Hughes
Methodistiaeth Galfinaidd Dinbych (1936) E Percy Jones
Crwydro Gorllewin Dinbych (1969) Frank Price Jones
Cofiant Thomas Gee (1913) T Gwynn Jones
The Streets of Denbigh (1981) R M Owen
The Diocese of St Asaph (1908) D R Thomas

Minutes of the Denbigh Borough Council
Files of the Denbighshire Free Press
Rhaglen Swyddogol Eisteddfod Dinbych 1939
Transactions of the Denbighshire Historical Society, Nos 15, 19 & 22

SEGRWYD HALL c 1890

Another mansion worthy of mention is Segrwyd Hall, situated in the Lawnt. Currently owned by Denbigh solicitor, David Hooson, Segrwyd has, over the centuries, been in the occupation of several notable families - the Dolbens, the most prominent of whom was David, consecrated Bishop of Bangor in 1631; the Mostyns, including John Mostyn, who made an abortive attempt to develop a woollen industry in the Brookhouse, and John Meredith Mostyn, who eloped to Gretna Green with Mrs Hester Lynch Thrale's daughter Cecilia; Rhoda Broughton the eminent novelist and Edward Pryce Storey of Coppy Farm, brewer and property owner.

TREFEIRIAN.

TREFEIRIAN c 1910

Trefeirian is situated beyond the top end of Love Lane immediately following Plas Castell Lodge. This handsome dwelling was built for John Harrison Jones, proprietor of Harrison Jones, Chemist (now Royles). He was a leading Wesleyan Methodist lay preacher and was elected Mayor of Denbigh in 1881 and 1882. He was primarily responsible for organising the huge 1884 Franchise Demonstration which took place in the field opposite Trefeirian and at which the principal speaker was the Rt. Hon. Joseph Chamberlain. At the Denbigh National Eisteddfod of 1882, Harrison Jones was Chairman of the Executive Committee. Trefeirian is now the social club for the employees of the North Wales Hospital.

YSTRAD ISAF. DENBIGH.

YSTRAD ISAF c 1920

Ystrad Isaf, owned by Doctors Gwyn and Marie Thomas, was the dower house of Ystrad Hall (now demolished) and the dower track between the two houses is still outlined by a yew hedge. Edward Hubbard in his book, Buildings of Wales - Clwyd, describes Ystrad Isaf as dating from the late 17th or early 18th century. Ordnance Survey maps show a Roman Road crossing one of the paddocks fronting the house. This was the line of the main road before the present road between the entrance to Ystrad Farm and the bridge below Ystrad Isaf. During World War 1 the Misses Hughes adapted the house as a Red Cross Hospital for wounded soldiers.

3

SALISBURY PLACE c 1920

Salisbury Place in Vale Street was the residence of Evan Pierce, an eminent local doctor and Coroner for West Denbighshire. He was Mayor of Denbigh from 1866 to 1870 and in 1876 a statue in his memory was erected opposite his home. After Dr Pierce's death in 1895, his widow lived there until her death in 1932. During World War 2, the St. John's Ambulance Brigade occupied part of the building. Plans by the Denbigh Borough Council to adapt the house as a municipal headquarters never materialised and, having fallen into disrepair, it was demolished in 1953. The site was cleared and Marsden's Biscuit factory was built there, to later become an Elizabeth Ann factory. In recent times the site was again cleared and a Gateway Supermarket erected.

PLAS CASTELL CLOCK TOWER 1922

This imposing clock tower was built by John Roberts, Contractor, Plough Inn, as an extension to Plas Castell. The foundation stone of the tower was laid on January 18th 1882 by the owner, Miss Emily Augusta Fazackerley, whose principal home was Banwell Abbey in Somerset. Plas Castell subsequently became the property of Sir D S Davies, M.P., son in law of Thomas Gee, and it eventually became a residence for Howell's School pupils. During 1884, Miss Fazackerley installed a tenant at Plas Castell and returned permanently to Banwell Abbey. The clock was removed by its maker, Henry Joyce, and installed in the tower of Banwell Parish Church. This postcard view was posted in 1922, showing another clock had been installed, but by today the tower is again clockless.

CLOCK TOWER PLAS CASTELL DENBIGH.

GWAENYNOG HALL c 1930

Gwaenynog Hall, situated a mile west of Denbigh, was the former Myddleton house. There is an ex situ date inscription of 1571 but in 1870, following the change of ownership to the Burton family, and again in 1914, major alterations were effected. On the Gwaenynog Estate are Johnson's Cottage and Johnson's Monument, so named because during 1774, Dr Samuel Johnson, a friend of Col. John Myddleton, spent some time as a guest at the Hall. It was at Gwaenynog also that Beatrix Potter spent many enjoyable holidays with her uncle, Frederick Burton, and found in the house and gardens the inspiration for some of her children's stories.

ST. HILARY'S CHURCH c 1885

This rare photograph of the interior of St. Hilary's was taken about 1885. Built during the 14th century, St. Hilary's served as both garrison and town church. In 1874, St. Mary's Church was built as a replacement but the main body of St. Hilary's was not demolished until 1923, leaving only the tower. William Ellis, who carried out the demolition, salvaged some of the materials to construct the bungalow known as Coriander. The beautiful brass chandelier, dated 1753, seen on the right, and a communion table dated 1628, were among the items taken to St. Marcella's. In the background is the gallery from where the orchestra accompanied the singing and chanting. The ownership of the box pews shown was usually confirmed by pew deed.

7

CAPEL MAWR c 1910

This Edwardian postcard view shows Capel Mawr Calvinistic Methodist Chapel at the junction of Beacon's Hill with Chapel Street. It was known at one time as Middle Chapel because of its position between Swan Lane Independent Chapel and Pendref Wesleyan Chapel. The original chapel, erected in 1793, and subsequently enlarged and remodelled, recently celebrated its 200th anniversary. With a seating capacity of 1000, Capel Mawr is one of the largest nonconformist places of worship in North Wales. Many eminent persons have been associated with the chapel, including Thomas Gee, publisher, Kate Roberts, novelist, Gwilym R Jones and Mathonwy Hughes, bards and journalists, and Frank Price Jones, lecturer and author.

COMMEMORATION SERVICE 1910

This rare postcard scene shows the congregation leaving St. Mary's Church after a commemorative service to King Edward VII taken by Canon Redfern, Rector of Denbigh. Despite an appeal by the Mayor, Alderman John Humphrey Jones, for the congregation to wear mourning, at least one lady is dressed in white. In the far right, Howell's School pupils are seen leaving the church via a side door. Top left is part of the wall which surrounded the old Hand Inn. On the right is the wall of the Lenten Pool Tannery on the site of which the Church Institute was built in 1916.

CHILDREN ATTENDING PROCLAMATION 1938

The schoolchildren of Denbigh are here assembled on the High Street prior to marching through Lenten Pool and up Smithfield Road to the Gorsedd field where the 1939 National Eisteddfod was to be proclaimed. The National School banner is carried by two senior boys and beneath the word Dinbych is seen Ella Edwards, who has charge of the pupils of the Infants Department lined up behind. From R to L the Infant children at the front, behind the banner are - Jean Roberts, Gracie Andrews, Alan Studholme, Tom Rogers, Parry Marshal and Enid Jones. Denbigh is decorated for the occasion and there is a profusion of bunting with several children carrying Y Ddraig Goch. During the morning the weather was unfavourable but it improved considerably by the time of the ceremony.

FLORAL DANCERS, 1938

Seen here are the 24 schoolgirls having just performed the Floral Dance at the Proclamation of the 1939 Denbigh National Eisteddfod which took place at the Gorsedd field off Lôn Llewelyn on Thursday, 7th July, 1939. The traditional sheaf of corn - Yr Aberthged - was carried by Elizabeth Roberts of Rhewl. The girls were trained by Josephine Jones, Headmistress of Frongoch Infants School, who herself inaugurated the dance, assisted by Annie Evans, teacher. This photograph was taken by Ronald Thompson on the putting green, just inside the main gates of the Lower Park Recreation Ground, with the Ruthin Road houses in the background.

NATIONAL EISTEDDFOD 1939

Shown here is the Pavilion for the National Eisteddfod of 1939 in process of erection by L. Woodhouse & Co., Contractors of Nottingham, on the Berllan fields off St. David's Lane. Seen in the background are the buildings of Howell's School and St. David's Church. The Gorsedd ceremonies were held in the field now occupied by the Bryn Stanley Estate on Lôn Llewelyn. A feature of the Denbigh Eisteddfod was that neither the Chair nor the Crown was awarded. The Chairman of the Executive Committee was William Jones, later Sir William of Ruthin, with Morris T. Williams, husband of Dr Kate Roberts, as General Secretary.

BOROUGH MARKETS 1909

The Denbigh Borough Market in Crown Square was opened in 1848. To the left is Miller's Pot Shop, which was erected on the site of the old Feathers Inn, demolished in 1849. To the right is Bellamy's Antique Showroom, a temporary business on the premises of the Farmer's Inn, closed in 1908. In the market entrance, on the left, are seen Joe Bartley and his uncle Edward James Edgar, and on the right, John Edgar, a well known fishmonger in the town. The market by-laws are displayed at the entrance. The ornate stonework above the entrance was resited on the old Butter Market entrance opposite the Foundry Garage in Chapel Place.

ASSEMBLY ROOMS c 1910

The Assembly Rooms were located above the old Cheese and Butter Market in Factory Place. Erected in 1843 as part of the Denbigh Borough Market Scheme, the rooms were let for a variety of activities including property sales, dramatic performances, political meetings and temperance rallies. The Assembly Rooms were taken down when the markets were demolished in 1914, prior to the building of the Town Hall in 1916. In recent years the remaining ground floor section has been used for storage and paper salvage by the council. It is currently occupied by Dyffryn Clwyd Brewery. The notice on the second door reads 'Sand for sale, apply Evan Evans Carrier.'

ANNEXE TO ASSEMBLY ROOMS c 1910

This stone building, contemporary with the old Borough Markets, stood against the gable end of the Assembly Rooms, which were above the old Butter Market (now Dyffryn Clwyd Brewery), and at the top of the steps which still lead from the Town Hall car park down to Chapel Place. The building itself was used primarily as an annexe to the Assembly Rooms and also as a base for the Toll Collector at the markets. This block, consisting of the Assembly Rooms and Annexe, was demolished in 1914 and the space formed has since been used for car parking. The advertisements are for - Spratts Dog Cakes; a sale at Densons; an L.N.W. Railway Excursion to the Fire Brigade Sports at Ruthin and Williams's Amusements including Hoopla.

CORPORATION REFUSE LORRY 1930's

This fine picture from the 1930's shows the new refuse lorry commissioned by the Sanitary Department of the Denbigh Corporation. Previously the collection of household refuse was carried out by horse and cart. The body work of this lorry was built on a chassis by Messrs Davies and Hughes, Coachbuilders of Vale Street, at their premises at the rear of the present Cellar Five off licence. This postcard view by Ronald Thompson, was taken in the old Horse Market in Smithfield Road, near the site of the present Fire Station. At the rear are seen the open fronted shelters where in times past horses were tethered and displayed for sale.

DENBIGH BOROUGH COUNCIL 1948

Read all names from *right to left*

Front Row - Clr. Lewis Williams; Clr. J L Jones; Clr. Eunice M Evans; Ald. J Hywel Owen; Henry Jones (Town Clerk); Ald. W D Pierce (Mayor); Ald. H M Lewis; Ald. Robert Hughes; Clr. John Jones; Clr. Caradog Rees; Clr. R Freeman Evans.

Second Row - Dr J T Lewis (Medical Officer); Clr. Emrys Roberts; Clr. Gwilym R Jones; Harry Jones; Richard Ll Jones; Thomas Ll Jones; (Mace Bearers and Bailiffs); Clr. E W Jones; Clr. Emlyn Maddocks; Clr. M J Tudor.

Back Row - Alun Hughes (Sanitary Dep't); D K Roberts (Finance Dep't); Howel Smith (Rent Collector); E Parry Davies (Admin.); Idris Lloyd (Admin.); M E Morris (Sanitary Inspector); D E Roberts (Press); W T Williams (Treasurer); R Alwyn Roberts (Surveyor); Alfred Roberts (Rating Officer).

17

DRUID INN c 1898

This interesting photograph dating from the turn of the century was taken outside the Druid Inn in Highate, now Evan Jones & Son, Electricians. At the horse's head is Robert Edwards, carrier at the North Wales Hospital and grandfather to R E Rowlands of Henllan who was a County Councillor for 33 years. In the doorway of the inn are David John Jones, licensee, and his wife. To the rear there was stabling accommodation for 12 horses. Immediately below the inn is Robert Owen's grocery shop. The Druid opened in 1812 and was closed at the Licensing Sessions of 1900. At the time of closure, evidence was given by the Denbigh Temperance Association 'that the bulk of the trade is derived from drunkards, poachers, thieves and loafers.'

STAR INN c 1900

Shown here is the Star Inn, High Street, at about the turn of the century when the licensee was Mrs Elizabeth Jones, licensed to sell Ale, Porter, Wines and Spirits. This inn gave its name to the adjoining grocer's shop owned by Robert Owen and was absorbed into the shop when the licence was lost. In 1853 the licensee, Hugh Hughes, was a faithful deacon at Swan Lane Chapel. An indication of the high number of inns in Denbigh a century ago is that the premises to the left of the Star was the Harp Inn whilst that to the right of Star Shop was the Druid.

FARMERS ARMS 1901

This postcard view addressed to Richard Roberts of the Farmers Arms bears a message stating that the picture was taken in September 1901. This inn occupies part of the site of the present Town Hall and the sign outside shows it to be owned by Salt and Co., who retailed Burton Ale and Stout. Previous to 1856 the Farmers Arms was known as the Three Wolves' Heads. The Crown Hotel which gives its name to the square, is one of the oldest inns in Denbigh, a reference in the Chirk Castle Accounts refers to John Hughes, The Crown, 1723. John Williams, Glanmor, in Ancient and Modern Denbigh (1856) wrote critically of the 'time killing loungers who sit in conference at the base of the Cross.'

HAWK AND BUCKLE HOTEL 1903

The Hawk and Buckle in Vale Street, originally known as The Falcon, was one of the oldest inns in Denbigh. The most interesting feature was the cockpit at the rear, dating from the second half of the 17th century, which in 1968 was removed to St. Fagan's Folk Museum in Cardiff. Another popular attraction in times past was the Bowling Green, from where the Rev. Thomas Charles of Bala once preached a sermon. Edwin Joseph Price, here described as a Wine and Spirit Merchant, was licensee from 1903 to 1907, when John Godfrey Lloyd, brother to Robert W Lloyd of the Bull Hotel, began a 50 year period as landlord. The inn recently closed and is being converted into flats.

BULL HOTEL c 1910

There is evidence in the Chirk Castle Accounts that the Bull was re-built in 1666. At one time known as the Black Bull and also the Guildhall Tavern, because of its proximity to the Shire Hall, the Bull has long been one of Denbigh's premier inns. Traditionally the Bull was regarded as a Tory house, while the Liberals were associated with the Crown. Shown standing in front is the horse drawn Bull bus which, at the Railway Station, competed with the Crown bus for custom. Wearing a bowler hat is Robert Lloyd, the proprietor, whose family owned the Bull from 1850 to 1943. As befits an old coaching inn, it contains an old carriage pole and swingle bars, a whip and coaching horns.

DRURY'S TEMPERANCE HOTEL c 1916

Drury's Temperance Hotel advertised by the illuminated sign above the door was just below the arched entrance to Garfield Terrace in Vale Street. It was kept by William Drury who was a staunch churchman, being sidesman and warden at St. David's Church. His strongly held views on Temperance were reflected in those days by the preference of many like minded persons, who preferred to stay at establishments where alcohol was not sold. Conveniently located near Denbigh Station, this hotel had a regular trade. It later became a greengrocer's shop, kept by Blodwen Lloyd and her sister, and because of the sound of the door bell, known as Siop Ding Dong.

BOER WAR VETERANS, 1902

The Peace Treaty ending the Boer War was signed on May 31st, 1902. Some weeks later, these weary troops, pictured in Lenten Pool, were brought to Denbigh Station by train and from there carried up Vale Street in carts drawn by the Borough Traction Engine. The procession was accompanied by the Town Band, conducted by Bandmaster Charlie Humphreys. Many of the soldiers are seen to be bandaged. To the rear is the tanyard owned by A Lloyd Jones, to be demolished when the Church Institute was built in 1916 and the gable end of Brynffynnon, currently occupied by Dr. Gwyn Thomas and Partners and formerly the home of William Williams (Caledfryn).

R.W.F. MARKSMEN, 1904

Here are shown representatives of D Company, 1st Volunteer Battalion, Royal Welsh Fusiliers, winners of the Battalion Challenge Cup at Salisbury Plain Camp in August 1904. This trophy had been won by D Company for 2 years and in the team are shown - Back Row, L to R, Sgt. W Williams; Sgt. J O Thomas; Pte. Edward Hughes; Sgt. R Williams. Centre, the Officer Commanding, Lt. Clough and Sgt. Instructor Pays. Front, Cpl. T Lloyd and Sgt. Tommy Roberts. Membership of the Volunteers, with the attraction of a uniform, an annual camp and weekly parades was highly prized and there was keen competition for selection. The Drill Hall behind, (now Pot Black) opened in 1882 to replace the old Armoury in Love Lane, was the centre of all Volunteer activity.

LIVERPOOL TERRITORIALS, 1913

These Territorials with kit bags and rifles are lined up outside Denbigh station where they have just arrived from Liverpool and are preparing to march along Ruthin Road to the huge training camp at Myddleton Park. War clouds are gathering and the soldier who sent this postcard to Miss D Muskin of Hatfield, Bootle, on 2nd August, 1913, writes that there is scarcely any free time to be had. The advertisements on the wall fronting the L.N.W.R. Goods Depot announce a grand sale at Denson's Shop and that to the right of the officer proclaims the merits of Whitbread stout, to be had at Ashfords Grocers.

WORLD WAR I PRISONERS c 1915

This scene shows a group of heavily guarded German prisoners of war being marched through Lenten Pool on their way from Denbigh Station to Dyffryn Aled, Llansannan. The hostility of the onlookers, many of whose relatives and friends had suffered as a result of the war, can be sensed, and the journey along Henllan Street was reported as being particularly dangerous. The Church Institute, which was opened on March 6th, 1916 by the Bishop of St. Asaph, the Rt. Rev. G A Edwards, is in the process of being built. In the right foreground is part of the wall surrounding the old Hand Inn.

TELEGRAM GIRLS 1916

This unusual picture was taken during July 1916 in the yard at the rear of Denbigh Post Office. Shown from L to R are - Percy Carlyle, Vivienne Jones (later Mrs George Pierce), Thomas Edwin Morris and Fanny Jones. Tommy Morris and Percy Carlyle were the official telegram boys based at Denbigh Post Office and, following their call up for military service, the two girls were appointed as their deputies. Sadly, Tommy Morris was killed on active service on 1st June, 1918 and he is commemorated on the plaque at the Post Office entrance. Percy Carlyle returned safely and resumed his career in the Postal Service.

HOME GUARD c 1942

Seen here is a picture of the L.M.S. Platoon, B Company of the 2nd Denbigh Home Guard during World War 2, taken on the platform at Denbigh Station. From L to R rear - Harold Ewer, sheds foreman; Ernie Jones, engine driver; Jackie Thomas, guard; a railway employee from Rhyl; Lt. Albert Crump, goods office; Arthur Jones, wheel tapper; Hugh Hughes, signalman. front - a guard from Rhyl; Charlie Griffiths, engine driver. The Platoon attended lectures at the Drill Hall and practised rifle shooting at Bryntrillyn. Their Home Guard duties were carried out in the vicinity of the station.

MAY DAY 1903

This fine picture shows Denbigh May Queen for 1903, Howell's School pupil, Elizabeth Adams, daughter of Richard Brittain Adams, County Surveyor, of Holland House, Lenten Pool. The carriage, beautifully decorated, was loaned for the occasion by the Burton family at Gwaenynog. In attendance are the train bearer, Robert Kitchen, and the driver, Tommy Williams of the Armoury, Love Lane. Angel's Vaults, (now Barclay's Bank), which closed in 1914, had an extensive brewery at the rear. To the left is Fred Williams's Haircutting Salon (now Vale Insurance).

MAY DAY 1932

Shown at the top of Henllan Street during the 1932 May Day Procession is John Morris Owen's Vulcan lorry carrying a representation of the cast who had performed the operatta 'Tangles' the previous winter. This was the first production of the Denbigh Amateur Dramatic and Operatic Society which had been formed by Josephine Jones, Frongoch School and Howel Smith, a Council Rating Official. Standing is Percy Freeman, with sisters May and Susie Williams, Fron Shop, and Rhoda Royles seated behind. Other productions by the Society included Slave in Araby, Gypsy Love and Vagabond King. The property on the left in this picture was owned by the Pilling family and the entrance next to it was Entry Fawr which led to three cottages. On the extreme right is Capel Seion.

MAY DAY 1933

Seen here is 1933 May Queen Rene Vaughan placing a wreath on the Denbigh War Memorial. She is accompanied by her six train bearers, arranged in pairs - Mary Roberts (Cotton Hall) and Nancy Fenwick Jones, Dora Yeardsley and Joyce Chambers Jones, Yvonne Sykes and Nerys Benson Evans. Bringing up the rear are the pages, Tecwyn and Sydney Johnson. Sydney is bearing the crown with which Queen Rene was later crowned by Mrs Goronwy Griffith. The taller girl to the rear is Alice Welburn of Groes Hall Cottage, who was the 1932 May Queen. Beside her is the Rev. J O Roberts, Rector of Henllan and President of the May Day Committee.

1933 MAY DAY PRIZE WINNER

During the 1933 May Day festivities, the various competitions were judged in the Horsemarket off Smithfield Road where the Fire Station is now situated. Seen here is the winning entry for 'a tradesman's motor lorry or van, loaded according to trade.' Standing on the running board is Stan Mortimer and in the driver's seat is Bert Roberts. Mellards in Crown Square, for many years the leading ironmongery business in Denbigh, was founded by William Mellard of Whitehall, Borough Mayor in 1895 and 1896. Behind the lorry is the gable end of Maeshyfryd Terrace and on the right is the Smithfield Garage. In pre-war days, the Horsemarket was a popular venue for funfairs.

1934 MAY DAY PARADE

Here is shown part of the 1934 May Day procession led by the May Queen, Beryl Pierce, in her decorated limousine, flanked by eight girl guides. Walking behind is Mrs Florrie Boyes with her sons, Stephen and Alfie, the former dressed as a Pearly King and the latter as a Battered Boxer. Vale Street is en fete for the occasion, the shops from the left being - Hepworths, Drapers; WH Smith, Newsagent; and The Denbigh Gas and Coke Company, followed by the County Court Offices. The crowning ceremony performed by Mrs Turnour took place at the castle, followed by a display of maypole dancing.

1934 VISIT OF COTTON QUEEN

On Thursday 30th August, 1934, the Cotton Queen of Lancashire, Gwladys Wood, visited Denbigh during the campaign to promote Lancashire cotton and thus relieve distress in the cotton towns. She was welcomed by the Mayor, Alderman John Morris Jones, and May Queen Beryl Pierce, who was attended by her pages, Billy Davies and Bobby Williams. The Mayoress, Mrs Pickwell, presented the Cotton Queen with a bouquet and the May Queen also bestowed a gift. After visiting Denson's emporium, the party proceeded to John Thomas and Sons, Drapers, where they were entertained to refreshments before continuing to Ruthin.

THOMAS GEE PRESENTATION 1895

This picture was taken at Plas Castell in 1895 after the presentation of a national testimonial to Thomas Gee (1815-1898). Thomas Gee was the publisher of the leading Welsh newspaper, Baner ac Amserau Cymru, and a prominent Liberal in both national and local politics. Mayor of Denbigh in 1871-72 and again in 1877-78, he was the first Chairman of Denbighshire County Council. Plas Castell was the home of Thomas Gee's son in law, David Saunders Davies, a prominent Manchester businessman and subsequently Liberal M.P. for the Denbigh Division. Among several prominent persons present are David Lloyd George, M.P. and Tom Ellis, M.P. 7th and 8th respectively from the right in the 3rd row, and Lord Clwyd, seated to the left of Mrs Gee.

FIRE BRIGADE 1903

Taken in 1904 this picture shows a splendid turnout of the Denbigh Fire Brigade with Driver Tommy Williams, The Armoury, at the reins. The Fire Station was at the Park Street end of the Bull Hotel, where an archway leads into the yard. In 1897 Robert Wynne Lloyd of the Bull Hotel was appointed Captain of the Brigade. The Lieutenants were John Morris Davies and W G Helsby, with L Sayle, H Miller and Roger Price as Engineers. The steam engine was supplied by Messrs Merryweather. To the rear is the old established Chemists shop of Harrison Jones (now Royles). To the right is one of two drapers shops in the town owned by T J Williams.

VETERAN CARS c 1906

Veteran car enthusiasts will recognise LC 3435 as a De Dion Bouton and this Registration Number dates from May 1905, issued by the old London County Court. K944 is a Napier and the Registration Number was issued in Liverpool from December 1903. The respective owners cannot be traced because in both instances the records were destroyed by enemy action during World War 2. This particular occasion is not known but the flags and bunting suggest a festive occasion, possibly May Day. The probability is that these motorists were simply passing through Denbigh and that an enterprising photographer took advantage of what was then an unique opportunity.

VALE STREET - FUNERAL 1913

The postcard depicting this funeral was posted in 1913. The coffin, having passed out of the picture, is escorted by helmeted members of the Town Fire Brigade, suggesting that the deceased was a member of that organisation. Members of the family are carried in the closed carriages and the rear of the cortege is brought up by members of the Volunteer Battalion. Vale Street is lined with onlookers, many of whom seem more interested in the photographer and his camera. On the far side, below the junction with Station Road, is Pyracantha House and above the junction can be seen the outline of Salisbury Place.

OPENING OF TOWN HALL 1916

Despite the rigours of World War I, this large crowd has assembled in Crown Square to witness the official opening of the New Town Hall. Previously the site had been occupied by the Borough Markets and the Farmers Arms Inn. Municipal and public functions had previously taken place at the County Hall, the Drill Hall and the Assembly Rooms. Standing on the balcony, from where the photograph was taken, are the Mace Bearers and Bailiffs. Among the crowd are the ancestors of many of our present townspeople. Outside the Crown Hotel is the Crown bus, a horse drawn carriage which conveyed hotel patrons to and from the Railway Station.

DENBIGH CRICKET CLUB 1923

Seen here are the representatives of the Denbigh Cricket Club who played against Northop during the 1923 season. In the match, which Denbigh won, J H Evans, the Captain, scored 32 runs and D E Williams took 5 for 21. This was the inaugural season of the North Wales League which saw Denbigh finish as runners up to St. Asaph with an equal number of points but a lower percentage.

Back Row - J H Morris, (Railway Clerk); Moses Parry, (Mechanic); D Ll (Glyn) Pierce, (Schoolmaster); H Davies, (Priest); P Phillips, (Bank Clerk) Umpire.
Seated - G V Humphreys, (Solicitor); C P Jones (Bank Official); J H Evans (Bank Manager); D E Williams, (Shopkeeper); F Levesley, (Licensee, Masons Arms). Front - I Ll Roberts, (Carpenter) and E A Perkins, (Bank Clerk).

This year Denbigh Cricket Club celebrates its 150th anniversary.

ROYAL VISIT 1923

On the 23rd November, 1923, the Prince of Wales, subsequently Duke of Windsor, visited Denbigh. The dais in front of the County Hall, constructed by Davies and Hughes, Coachbuilders, was erected by David Lloyd of The Timber Yard. A space had been cleared in front of the dais to accommodate ex servicemen and schoolchildren. The Prince was welcomed by the Mayor, Goronwy Griffith, who, on behalf of the Borough, presented a Loyal Address in Welsh. The Prince then proceeded to the War Memorial where he received from Private T R Jones, a severely disabled ex-serviceman, a wreath of laurels, which he placed on the Memorial. The Lord Lieutenant then introduced the Royal Visitor to the Council Members and Officials. The entourage then departed for Ruthin.

TOWN BAND c 1932

In this Helsby postcard, the members of the Denbigh Town Band during the early thirties are grouped outside the Town Hall entrance. The Bandmaster, J O Thomas, is 5th from the left in the second row. The cannon behind the railing is a Russian memento from the Crimean War (1853-56). In August, 1940, it was given to the National Appeal for Scrap Iron. On the wall above is the plaque, commemorating the building of the New Town Hall, laid on the 25th March, 1915 by Thomas Lloyd Jones, Mayor. The placard on the right shows the films to be shown at the Enterprise Cinema, in the Town Hall, during the week when the picture was taken.

DENBIGH LIBERAL CLUB – ALTERATIONS COMMITTEE 1930's

Front Row - R G Jones; D Webbe Davies; J L Jones; Morgan Davies; Emrys Jones; Robert Owen; W J Williams; David Jones.

Second Row - J J Evans; Alun Gough Roberts; D Wheway Davies; R Oliver Davies; William Humphreys; H Marsden Davies.

Third Row - George Lloyd; Elwy Owen; Peter John Thomas; D E Roberts; Gwilym Lloyd.

Back Row - D O Griffiths; Jack Rogers; Goronwy Owen; Trefor Jones; Jim Roberts; Dei Ellis; J Wesley Evans; Hugh Lloyd Jones; J Evans; John Hughes.

For many years until its closure in 1955, the Liberal Club occupied the rooms above E B Jones, Grocers (now Lloyds Supersave Drugstore).

THARK AT NORTH WALES HOSPITAL 1940

Seen here is the cast of the Denbigh Amateur Operatic and Dramatic Society which performed the comedy Thark at the North Wales Hospital Theatre in February 1940. Proceeds were earmarked for The Red Cross Local Comforts Fund. From L to R members of the cast are - Eileen Gamble; Herbert Roberts; Dora Roberts; Sam Vaughan Williams; Percy Freeman; Stan Rees; Rhoda Royles; Dick Owen; Cissie Jones; M Owen (Dedwyddfa) and T Roberts (Bodfari). The Producer was Josephine Jones and the Stage Manager Howell Smith. Musical interludes were played by the Hospital Orchestra conducted by Dr Frank Jones.

BROOKHOUSE FARM FIRE 1940

During August 1940, Denbigh Fire Brigade under Captain R T Williams and the Auxiliary Fire Service under Patrol Leader D Wheway Davies, were engaged continuously for 27 hours at Brookhouse Farm fighting this serious conflagration. Whilst unloading hay, heat from the exhaust of a tractor caused some wisps of hay to ignite and in a very short time a bay of hay was ablaze. Neighbouring farmers and their workmen gave every assistance possible, but according to the occupant, Robert Hughes, over 40 tons of hay and many implements were destroyed. This dramatic postcard is a fine example of the opportunism of Ronald Thompson.

TOWER HILL c 1900

This early picture of Tower Hill has no houses on the right hand side and neither Leicester Terrace nor St. Hilary's Terrace has been built. The castellated building on the left is said by John Williams in Ancient and Modern Denbigh to have been an Elizabethan inn. Burgess Tower, lower down the hill, dates from the 14th century and was the entrance to the old town within the town walls. For many years, the tower was the council chamber of the town burgesses. It also served as a prison and as a repository for municipal documents.

H. M. STANLEY COTTAGES c 1903

This interesting postcard published by Edgar incorporates a frontal view of Denbigh Castle with the two cottages with which the early life of Henry Morton Stanley was associated. The cottage on the right, now demolished, occupied a site corresponding with the now defunct Stanley Bowling Green. This was where the eminent explorer, christened John Rowlands at nearby St. Hilary's Church, was born on 28th January, 1841, the illegitimate son of Elizabeth Parry. At the age of 5, the child was placed in the care of Richard and Jenny Price who lived in Bowling Green Cottage to the left of the Castle entrance. The following year he was taken to the workhouse at St. Asaph where he remained for nine years.

GOBLIN TOWER AND COTTAGE c 1903

Goblin Tower does not derive its name from any connection with hobgoblins or the like. Gobelin is a well known French surname and it may well be the name of a person involved in the building of the tower. The well in the tower - known as The Bloody Well - is thought to be that into which Henry de Lacy's eldest son fell to his death. The cottage, inhabited up to the turn of the century by a celebrated local taxidermist, Hugh Richards and his family, has long since been demolished.

41 TO 45 HIGH STREET c 1900

The horses and cart shown here are from Cae'r Mynydd Farm, Saron. The Post Office in the centre (No 43 High Street), now the Chinese Restaurant and previously Trefor Davies, Fish and Chip Restaurant, had by 1905 moved to its present position near the County Hall. To the left is the shop of David Hughes described as Boot and Shoe Manufacturer, now Clough and Co Auctioneers, and before that Hughes Fishmongers. To the right of the picture is the old established (1849) grocery of Thomas Roberts, Tanswan, thus named because of its original location below the Swan Inn in Vale Street. Tanswan Shop was demolished following a disastrous fire in 1982.

HIGH STREET LOOKING WEST c 1903

This postcard in the Wrench series was posted in April, 1904. The shops on the south side from R to L are - E B Jones, Grocer, with the Liberal Club above, Hookes Kennard, Chemist, and Densons Drapers. Andrew's Vaults is described as Wine and Spirit Merchant, Importer, Bonder and Dealer and Retailing Bass's Ales and Guinness's Extra Stout. The Vaults dates back to 1779 and, before the Smithfield Market was opened in 1895, cattle were sold on the High Street from a squared area fronting the inn. In the middle distance, the Conservative Club and the shops below, erected in 1891, are comparatively recent buildings.

HIGH STREET c 1924

This postcard view by Kingsway shows a typical High Street scene in Denbigh between the Wars. Despite the absence of market stalls, the popularity of the town as a shopping centre is clearly evident. Prominent features include Tanswan Shop on the left advertising Hovis Bread and the vertical sign on the far right advertising Bradleys Men's Outfitters. The gas lamp in front of Siop Pwmp (now Siop Clwyd) stands approximately where the old High Street water pump was located. The steps with handrails lead to the Harp Inn (closed 1927) and the clock on the wall above Keepfer's shop next door is clearly visible. Note that the shops on the northerly side of the street have their window blinds out for protection from the sun.

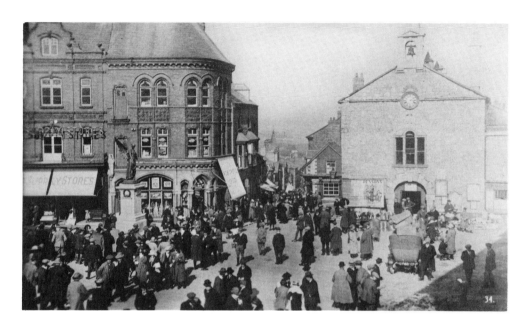

THE SQUARE AND WAR MEMORIAL c 1924

Another superb Kingsway card published in the same series as the previous picture. Again the eastern end of High Street fronting the County Hall shows a considerable gathering of shoppers. The solitary motor vehicle EY 150 causes minimal obstruction and most of the people have ample time to stand and gossip. The War Memorial, recently erected in 1923, appears to be a particularly popular meeting place. The window blinds in both Star Supply and Clwyd Pierce shop are evident and the hoarding in front of the County Hall is almost completely taken up by a large Densons advertisement. The old established (1840) butcher's shop of Thomas Davies, since demolished, can be seen at the top of Vale Street.

HIGH STREET - MARKET STALLS c 1936

This scene, with the market stalls down the centre, has been the pattern on Wednesdays in Denbigh High Street for many years. The shoppers appear to be warmly clad against the wintry weather and seem to have ample time to stand and gossip with the shelter of the Piazza proving a popular refuge. There is little demand for parking space and the policemen on the right have no urgent matters needing their attention. Once familiar items which have since disappeared include the street lights suspended above the centre of the street and the weighing machine outside D Morris, Chemist, known as Medical Hall.

LOWER VALE STREET c 1905

During the early years of this century, Vale Street was not tarred and the Corporation water cart was in regular use to keep the dust down. On the corner of Station Road is W H Smith's newsagents, having lost out to Wymans for the contract to maintain a stall on the station platform. Below is the wall of Pyracantha House where the road sweeper has time to stand and stare. On the left is Williams's Hairdressing Salon and Stationery Shop - later held by Meadowcroft and R Morris and currently R S McColl. Next is John Roberts's Grocery Shop where David John Pierce and J P Davies followed, at present occupied by Cellar 5. The house beyond, now known as Rhewl Goch, advertises Good accommodation for Cyclists.

UPPER VALE STREET c 1910

Yet another excellent Kingsway postcard of the upper part of High Street with Bronallt, once the home of Thomas Gee, on the left. Subsequent to this picture the house was adapted as a shop for Hughes & Sons, Costumiers and Tailors. The next shop down is Evans, Confectioners, followed by T O Jones, Grocers. In the distance is the gable end of Bank Place Stores owned by C H Lewis and now, L. Rowland, Chemists. Top right is the shop of Connah's selling Pratt Oil and Premier Bicycles 'By Appointment to H M The King.' Next down is the plumbers business of S M Dalton, to be later taken over by Charles Boycott. Silhouetted against the King's Arms is a barber's pole. Most of the buildings on the right have been demolished to provide a shopper's car park.

THE PADDOCK c 1930

This rare view of The Paddock, Vale Street, shows the land upon which Ronald Thompson's Photography Studio (now Tai Clwyd Offices) was built. Shown gathering daffodils is the wife of AneurinO Evans, a prominent Denbigh solicitor. Across the road is Grove House, a well proportioned 18th century building, which includes part of a house built in 1574 by Hugh Clough, brother of the more famous Sir Richard. Once the home of Dr Turnour, it is now a form of sheltered accommodation. Next down is Whitehall, currently an Abbeyfield Society House and previously the Borough Council Offices. The house in its present form was built for William Mellard, Mayor of Denbigh, 1895-96 and subsequently purchased by Aneurin O Evans, himself Mayor during 1901-2.

THE COUNTY HALL c 1946

Erected during the 16th century on land donated by Robert Dudley, Earl of Leicester and substantially restored in 1780, the County Hall has provided a variety of uses as - council chamber, court of law, police lock-up and a venue for public gatherings. Market facilities were made available on the ground floor. The left hand window gives opening times of the Carnegie Library as - Mondays and Fridays, 6 p.m. - 8.30 p.m. and Wednesdays 2 p.m. to 4 p.m. The hoardings advertise films at the Scala Cinema and the pantomimes Aladdin and Red Riding Hood at the Queen's Theatre, Rhyl. The Denbigh Christmas Market is advertised and a poster calls on the local electorate to support John Morris Jones. Older readers will remember Lloydie Davies, the bill poster who serviced several similar hoardings in Denbigh.

ANWYL HUGHES TRAY PAINTING c 1852

The Anwyl Hughes tray painting from which this postcard has been produced - hence its oval shape - is in the possession of Dr. Gwyn Thomas and dates from about 1852. In the foreground is a tree lined Ruthin Road; the horseman is said to be Dr Turnour of Grove House, who later became Chief Medical Officer at Denbighshire Infirmary. The Infirmary, which was founded in 1807, is clearly identifiable as is the first St David's Church which was consecrated in 1840. However, neither Howell's School (1859) nor the Denbigh - Ruthin railway line is evident.

VIEW FROM GRAIG QUARRY c 1904

This impressive view taken from the top of the Graig Quarry is dated about 1904. To the left, at the upper end of Grove Road is Frongoch School, opened by the Denbigh School Board in 1877 as an Infants School. The original buildings of Denbigh County School for Boys, opened in 1903, show the Middle Lane Field to be undeveloped. The land at the bottom of Beacon's Hill below Fairfield is similarly void of buildings. Both schools were built by John Simon Roberts, Building Contractor, of the Plough Inn, Bridge Street. Lôn Copner or Doctor's Lane, which links Vale Street with Middle Lane, has not yet been opened.

PORTLAND PLACE AND BRIDGE STREET c 1908

This rare postcard view of Portland Place and Bridge Street gives a clear indication of the narrowness of the roadway before the street widening project accomplished in 1936. This necessitated the demolition of buildings on the north side thus enabling the present shops from Woolworths down to Cawthrays to be built. In this Edwardian view are seen from right to left - Leopard Inn; W A Homan's Barber Shop: W Roberts's Boot Shop and the Confectioner's shop and Refreshment Rooms known as Williams, Penyffordd. On the opposite side, below the Conservative Club, which was built some 17 years previously, the shop buildings remain unaltered. Below the sign Dunlop Tyres is Buller's Tobacconist and Cycle shop followed by the striped pole indicating Emmanuel's Hairdressing Salon.

MIDDLE LANE c 1910

An early postcard view of houses at the upper end of Middle Lane, so called because it lies between Beacon's Hill and Vale Street. The Eton collars and knickerbocker trousers worn by the boys indicate the period to be pre World War 1. The shuttered windows are a necessary safeguard against the cost of repairing broken window panes. The cobbled pavement, a feature of the period, has long since been replaced. During the 16th century, this roadway was known as King Street and is shown on Speed's map of 1610 to be an important thoroughfare.

POST OFFICE LANE c 1910

Another pre 1914 view of houses at the Vale Street end of Post Office Lane. The houses to the left were demolished by the Borough Council after World War 2 to allow for the opening of the Post Office Lane Car Park. From this end of the lane entries led into two courtyards of small cottages known as Courts 1 and 2. Contrary to popular belief, there has never been a Crown Post Office in this area. The Welsh version - Lôn Bostws - Post House Lane - gives the true derivation. The steep gradient of Vale Street made it necessary for horses drawing coaches to be changed at the rear entrance of the Hawk and Buckle Inn.

HENLLAN STREET c 1910

Seen at the doorway of their cottage at the bottom of Henllan Street, immediately above the shop once known as Cotton's, are Joseph Roberts, tailor and his granddaughter Edith Davies. Joseph Roberts plied his trade from his home and according to custom worked seated crosslegged on the kitchen table. These three cottages were demolished during the 1930's, the planned erection of a Salvation Army Citadel never being accomplished. Interesting period features in the picture include - guttering across the two dormer windows; a boot scraper outside the front door; shutters for a downstairs window; a baby wrapped in a shawl in the care of a young girl; a gas lamp which would be lit and extinguished by the lamplighter.

LENTEN POOL 1923

This view of Lenten Pool can be dated fairly accurately as being post 1923 - when the Cross was moved from Crown Square, and pre 1924 - when the Hand Inn was rebuilt. Lenten Pool is already a bus terminus for the Red Dragon Bus seen outside the old National School. The three ladies are believed to be Gwladys Price, Ella and Ruby Edwards, teachers at the school. The carter with his load of coal proceeding up Henllan Street is John Williams, Nevin. A plaque above the front door shows that the school opened in 1847 as a Blue Coat School. It closed in 1976 and the front has been preserved as the facade of a complex of flatlets for the elderly.

AERIAL VIEW, TOWER TERRACE AREA c 1935

This aerial view of the area to the south of Highgate and lower Love Lane is quite revealing. The Scala Cinema now The Futura in the centre, which replaced the old Armoury, has survived where several other cinemas have been forced to close. The buildings to the right of the cinema have been replaced recently by a terrace of houses and Tŷ Twrch, one of the oldest buildings in the town, seen here on the right of the junction of Love Lane with Swine Market, has been adapted as flats. The ten cottages in Tower Terrace are easily identifiable but the adjoining houses in Tan y Gwalia have long since been demolished. Tower Hill Congregational Chapel, built in 1872, the larger building in front of Burgess's Tower, is now a Masonic Hall.

PANTON HALL 1960's

This rare picture of Panton Hall taken before the demolition of the cottages on the right, shows on the near right the wall surrounding the builder's yard of William Ellis & Son. In the middle distance, against the gable end of Hennessey Terrace, is the small shop, since demolished, where Llewelyn Williams began his electrical business. Previously it was the workshop of Moses Jones, Bookbinder. Next is the gable end of the shop occupied by George Milan, Watchmaker and previously Royles, Confectioners. This has also been demolished. Panton Hall itself has long since disappeared and was probably the residence of John Panton, Architect, who was Recorder of Denbigh in Elizabethan times.

CROWN SQUARE 1905

This red bricked building on the corner of Crown Square was one of several buildings in the town built by John Roberts, Contractor, of the Plough Inn. On the left is Star Tea Company, a well known firm of multiple grocers, with Clwyd Pierce's delicatessen on the corner. Between them is sandwiched the office of Jones & Son, Coal merchants, which is 'Open Wednesdays and Fridays from 2 p.m. to 4 p.m.' A feature of High Street shops at this time is that incoming goods were raised to the storerooms on the upper floors by pulley. Above Clwyd Pierce's shop, on the roof ridge, the name is formed in decorative ironwork. The first shop in Vale Street is R G Jones's Drapery.

T A JOHNSON TOWNSEND 1909

This fine display of meat, not subject to current legislation regarding hygiene, is shown at the shop of Thomas Allen Johnson whose family for many years held the licence of the Railway Inn opposite. The shop, known as Colomendy House, was built by Mr Johnson's father in order that the Borough Magistrates would grant him a game licence. Previously they had refused to allow him to deal in game from the inn because of the possibility of encouragement to poachers. The beast displayed in front of the shop had just been awarded a prize at Byford's Auction in Ruthin. Standing on the left with arms folded is Joe Johnson. These premises are currently occupied by Clwyd Computers and were previously Glenys Jones, Greengrocer.

D W DAVIES c 1919

This gentlemen's outfitters shop, located at the westerly entrance to Back Row, and owned by D Webbe Davies, father of the late David Wheway Davies, O.B.E. is at present a Chinese restaurant. The window display is dominated by collars, cuffs and shirt fronts which would usually be starched stiff and worn with a Sunday best suit. As a young man, D Webbe Davies had trained for the tailoring trade and had served a period as a cutter with Messrs Bradleys at 24, High Street. Up to 1905, this shop was the site of the town's main Post Office before the present Post Office was built. D W Davies's shop was followed by Johnny Jones's Boot Store.

BEEHIVE SHOP 1920's

The Beehive Drapery, Nos 9 and 11 Vale Street, consisted of two shops, the upper shop, a gentlemen's outfitters (now a health shop), and the lower shop (now the Principality Building Society), catering for ladies. In this picture are seen, L to R - Griff Roberts, Owen Jones, Proprietor and his son John Lloyd Jones and the Misses Mary Williams, Phyllis Williams, Anne Jones and Gwen Williams. Above the gent's shop were the millinery and mantle rooms and above the lower shop were the living quarters. In October, 1932, the building was badly damaged by fire. The upper shop was later occupied by Paragon's drapery and the lower shop by Hunter's Grocers and Irish Linen Warehouse successively. The name Beehive came from the Beehive Inn which occupied the site during the 18th century.

ROBERT OWEN & SONS c 1925

Taken during the mid twenties, this picture shows some of the staff of Robert Owen &
Son, described here as Grocers, Provision, Corn and Flour Merchants. This extensive
business took the name Star Shop from the inn of that name which formerly occupied
part of the site. Above the shop were commodious living quarters and access to the busy
bakehouse was via a narrow entry on the right. Seen in the doorway are Ted Roberts and
John Owen and standing centre are D E Owen (Kelly) and John Davies (Faldy). On the
far right is A D Andrews who later opened his own grocer's shop in the Bridge Street
premises now known as The Gem. Star Shop has now become the Halifax Building
Society.

PRITCHARD'S GENT'S OUTFITTERS c 1925

Pritchard's Gent's outfitters department opened into Back Row. A wide variety of caps, ties, socks and shirts were displayed for sale with an advertisement offering 'Plus fours hand made to measure!' John Pritchard is shown in the doorway with assistant Miss Marad Jones of Tŷ Newydd Farm, Trefnant. The two boys are Bobby Pritchard, who became a leading veterinary surgeon in the town on the left, and his brother Arthur, who became a chemist based at Chester on the right. Rodney Williams of Bryn, Bull Lane is on the left. Above the shop is the office of the Welsh language newspaper, Baner ac Amserau Cymru, managed by the Rev. John Morris Jones. These premises are now part of the She fashion shop.

PRITCHARD'S OUTFITTERS c 1926

Here are John Pritchard and his wife Ellen outside their Ladies' and Gent's Outfitters shop under the Piazza at 19, High Street. The shop first opened for business on Wednesday, 23rd March, 1921, having replaced a tobacconist's shop which was associated with Medical Hall Chemists. John Pritchard had previously spent some years as a lighthouse keeper. On the left of Pritchard's, Price Jones kept a grocery shop and on the right, Messrs Dicks Footwear store are displaying men's shoes for sale at 12s 6d a pair. Between the shop windows is a Red Dragon bus time table and the tail end of one of William Edwards's buses can just be seen.

SIOP DWY FERCH c 1930

This postcard shows the cafe/confectionery shop on the south side of Bridge Street (No. 11) officially called Llwyn Derw but known more popularly as Siop Dwy Hen Ferch - shop of the two spinsters. Standing in the doorway on the left is Alice Jones, the proprietor and with her Margaret Parry. Alice Jones was a daughter of Cae Gronw Farm, Tanyfron, and her farming connections and the tasty food supplied ensured a steady flow of customers, particularly on Market and Fair Days. The shop immediately below was a fish and chip shop, kept by Hugh Davies, which he later converted into a cobbler's shop. Above was the butcher's shop of Pierce Davies. The cafe is now a clothing shop owned by Meirion Davies.

WILLIAMS BROTHERS c 1930

Williams Brothers, as it was generally known, was a well patronised grocery business in Henllan Place. Here, E H Williams, the proprietor, is standing in the shop doorway, and the large double doorway beyond led to the bakehouse, several outhouses and some fields. On the gable is the hoist by which sacks of flour and provisions were lifted into the warehouse. A doorway in the ivy covered wall led to the dwelling house known as Ivy House. The entire property, together with Ivy House, was demolished to facilitate the development of Llwyn Mair, Maes yr Eglwys and Accar y Forwyn Estates. On the left, near the lamp post, is the entrance to the Baptist Chapel graveyard.

J H MILLS, POT SHOP
c 1932

J H Mills's Pot Shop at 45, Vale Street, now Denis R Jones, Accountants, is decorated with flags and bunting for what may have been a May Day celebration during the 1930's. Here were sold all manner of crockery, glassware, hardware and household goods. J H Mills was a prominent townsman and was elected Councillor and subsequently Alderman of the Denbigh Borough Council. Higher up Vale Street is Cooledge's Boot and Shoe Repair Shop. In post war years it became Lindsay's Paint Shop and is currently Fagin's Book store. In the foreground is Roy Hughes of Henllan Street.

T O JONES & SONS c 1933

This unusual window display at 23, Vale Street, the Grocery shop of T O Jones & Sons was an entry for a nation wide competition held by Kiaora, the fruit juice company, during the 1930's. The display was prepared by Tom Hughes, the shop manager and involved the use of real turf and hedgerow materials. This old established (1886) grocery business, Telephone No. Denbigh 14, was started by Thomas Owen Jones, who developed his knowledge of the grocery trade while employed as a tea blender at Harrison Jones Chemists Shop (now Royles). His son Eddie then ran the shop until 1969. The premises are now occupied by The Charity Shop.

IRWINS 1933

This fine view of Irwins, the multiple grocers, with their headquarters at Kirkdale, Liverpool, dates from 1933. John Irwin & Sons Ltd. bought the old Harp Inn in 1927 from John Godfrey Lloyd of the Hawk and Buckle Inn and built their modern shop on the site. The property came into the ownership of Tescos, the supermarket chain, and currently the premises are occupied by Threshers, Wine Merchants. Among the advertisements shown are - sliced baked ham at 1s 8d per lb; Price's Lobster 8½d; Silver Spoon Tea from 1s 8d; Potted meat from 4½d; Stewed Plums 5d per lb; and Roll bacon 7½d per lb. An indication of the high unemployment prevalent during the 1930's is a notice stating 'Relief vouchers accepted here.'

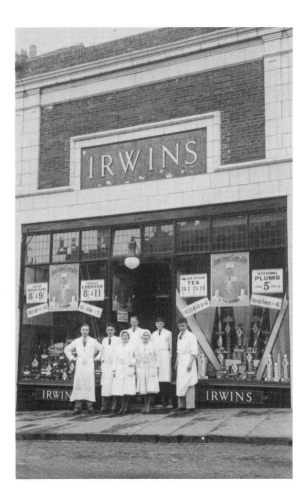

F W WOOLWORTHs 1935

Following the demolition of the buildings on the northerly side of Bridge Street during the street widening project of the 1930's, the first new shop to be erected was that of F W Woolworth & Co. Ltd., described as the 3d and 6d stores. The large window notices declare the opening to be at 9 a.m. on Friday, July 3rd, 1935. Taken from a position near the Conservative Club, the picture shows the shop in isolation, with the Graig fields beyond and the remains of Hughes, Pioneer Drapery on the right. In the right hand doorway is seen the late Dovey Pritchard.

JACK ROBERTS & SON GREENGROCER c 1936

This postcard view of Jack Roberts & Son's Greengrocery shop was taken on a festive occasion during the 1930's. Situated just below the Hawk and Buckle Inn in Vale Street, the shop was subsequently a men's hairdressing salon run by W Alsop. The late Jack Roberts was a prominent Denbighite, a founder member of the Denbigh Flower Show, and in company with the late Harry Ellis, raised thousands of pounds for charitable and patriotic purposes during World War II. The greengrocery tradition is being continued in the family by his grandson, Michel Roberts, at his shop in 46, High Street.

R E EDWARDS ICE CREAM c 1948

A familiar sight in Denbigh was the ice cream van of R E Edwards which, particularly during the summer months, toured the streets of the town. The clanging of his hand bell was the signal for children to leave their play and rush home for ice cream money. R E Edwards and his wife previously kept a shop in Caerwys and later opened a milk bar at 7, Vale Street (now Links Jewellery) where they also sold confectionery and greengroceries. Castle Ices were widely advertised as having won numerous diplomas. Other local ice cream vendors, before and after the war years, were Howel Royles and Stan Roberts, who plied their trade from special tricycles, and Auntie Winnie of 9, Ruthin Road (now Townsend Carpets).

CROWN SQUARE 1950's

This 1950's photograph by Ronald Thompson shows two former Denbigh shops in Crown Square, opposite the Crown Hotel. Shown on the left is the Imperial Wallpaper Company owned by P Bullock and Sons Ltd., and advertising the merits of Walpamur Products, Vesta Paints and Marvo Distemper. The adjoining stationery, confectionery and tobacconist shop, known popularly as Myddleton Bach, sold Wills Gold Flake and St. Julien Tobacco; Lucky Star, Capstan and Craven A cigarettes; Victory V Lozenges and Needlers Chocolates. The rendering on the walls has been removed to expose the heavy wooden beams of the original building. Both properties have since been absorbed into the She Fashion Shop.

TOWNSEND STEAM SAW MILLS c 1903

This fine Edwardian industrial scene is of the Townsend Steam Saw Mills and Timber Yard located at the junction of Vale Street and Rhyl Road. Esatblished in 1858 and previously known as the Vale of Clwyd Timber and Slate Company, the business was owned by the Roberts brothers of Claremont. The employees, five of whom are displaying circular saws of varying sizes, include, standing at the rear on the right, Morris Owen, yard foreman for 36 years and great grandfather of the author of this volume. These premises are currently occupied by Townsend Agricultural Supplies.

LÔN COPNER c 1903

This luggage cart built by Messrs Williams Bros., Coachbuilders, (now Love Lane Garage) is displayed in Lôn Copner or Doctor's Lane, which links Vale Street from Beech House Surgery with Middle Lane. The intended extension of Lôn Copner across the land which was once part of the County School, into Beacon's Hill, was never achieved. Williams Bros. had a high reputation for top class workmanship, and in the pre-motor car age, their services were in great demand. They employed carpenters, wheelwrights, painters, blacksmiths and upholsterers to produce carriages of all types - traps, gigs, phaetons, broughams and carts.

WHITE ROSE BUS DEPOT c 1925

In the early twenties, the White Rose Bus Company, owned by Joe Brookes of Rhyl and his brothers, developed a Rhyl/Denbigh bus service. By 1926 the company had built the bus depot at the rear of the old National School in Lenton Pool, on the site of a large garden associated with Liverpool House. By 1930 the White Rose Company had been taken over by Crosville. The pumps outside the garage advertise Shell, B.P. and Pratts. The school wall on the right is being realigned to widen the access to the garage. It is questionable whether the signs outside the house would be permitted under current planning regulations.

DENBIGH FOUNDRY
c 1903

Denbigh Foundry (now Foundry Garage) was in Chapel Place opposite the old Cheese and Butter market. The original Foundry began in a building adjacent to the Hand Inn in Henllan Place but the owners Thomas Roberts and Hugh Jones moved to Factory Place during the 1880's. During the period 1890-1910, under the direction of Col. T A Wynne Edwards of the Plas Nantglyn family, the enterprise prospered and upwards of 40 men were employed in a thriving engineering business. Wynne Edwards, here seen standing on the extreme left, was a man of inventive mind and among many items of machinery, developed and produced a successful type of plough. During 1890 and 1891 he was Mayor of Denbigh.

DENBIGH STATION c 1910

Lined up around the platform of Denbigh Station are some of the staff including the Stationmaster, guards, booking clerks, porters and cleaners. During the 1880's, the total number of station employees including drivers, firemen, signalmen and permanent way staff rose to 120, but by complete closure in 1968, the number had dwindled to single figures. The original Vale of Clwyd Railway, formed in 1858, was soon taken over by the London and North Western Railway, (seen above) and this in turn was absorbed by the London Midland Scottish Railway under the Railways Act of 1921. The boy holding the newspapers is T Artemus Jones who left the National School at the age of 11 and ended his career as a County Court Judge.

The Graig. Denbigh

THE GRAIG 1914

Limestone has been quarried commercially at the Graig Quarry since the seventeenth century. It is highly probable that some of the stone used in the building of Denbigh Castle (1282+) was painstakingly levered from rocky outcrops in the vicinity. In more recent times, as the demand for building stone decreased, lime burning and the production of tarmacadam provided a stimulus for the oldest industrial site in the borough. Records show that from 1705 up to the beginning of this century, the quarry and the farm, each forming part of the Plas Heaton Estate, were run as a joint venture by the occupants of the farm. This postcard view was published by Evan Jones, Druid Buildings.

CROSVILLE BUS 1930

This picture was taken at the lower end of Vale Street, near the old railway bridge which carried the Denbigh - Ruthin railway line and which was demolished in May 1971 after being struck by an excavator on the back of a low loader. This White Rose bus shown had recently been taken over by the Crosville Company. Neither the conductor, wearing the familiar cross belts for ticket machine and cash bag, nor the driver is uniformed. The ladder at the rear of the bus provided access to the roof where excess luggage was carried. It is a matter of conjecture whether the cigar smoking, knickerbockered figure near the gas lamp is Aneurin O. Evans, the well known Denbigh solicitor.

DAIMLER HEARSE 1930's

Another fine postcard of the Daimler hearse owned by the Denbigh Smithfield Garage and based at the garage at the bottom of Smithfield Road (now C J Williams Electrical Ltd.) The hearse was hired out to funeral undertakers and usually driven by Reg Dominey, Maeshyfryd, Joe Roberts, Gwaenynog Lodge, or Tom Evans, The Green. By the 1970's the Smithfield Garage Company, headed by R Kerfoot Owen also had showrooms in Vale Street (until recently Allitts) and filling stations at Abbey Garage and Castle View. Behind the hearse is the Church Institute with the ornamental railings around, which were to be removed during the World War 2 Scrap Metal Salvage Campaign.

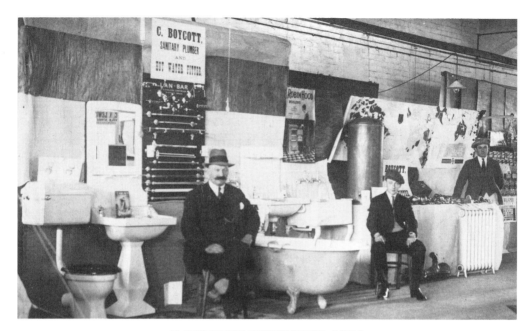

BOYCOTT PLUMBER 1935

This comprehensive display of bathroom fittings, central heating radiators and boilers at their Town Hall Market stand, is part of the stock available from the old established firm of Charles Boycott described here as a Sanitary Plumber and Hot Water Fitter. Seen here with his sons, Harold and Will, Charles Boycott had as a youth been apprenticed to S M Dalton at 10, Vale Street (now demolished) and in due course he took over the business. Apart from general plumbing and gas installations, Boycotts undertook all forms of glazing from their glass depot in Melling's Lane, and for some years Will Boycott dealt with repairs to stained glass windows at churches in the Diocese of St. Asaph.

GEE AND SON c 1937

This picture was taken at the rear of Messrs Gee and Son's premises in Chapel Street. Seen here from L to R are - Gwilym Roberts, machine attendant; Eddie Simon, Secretary; unknown; Aneurin Jones, handyman; and front, Jackie Pierce and Richard Roberts, both linotype apprentices. Jackie Pierce was killed on active service in 1944. The door to the left led to the small machine room where small miscellaneous items such as programmes and tickets were produced. The right hand door led to the bookbindery. The handcart in the foreground bearing the words North Wales Times was used by Aneurin Jones to convey bundles of North Wales Times and Y Faner down Beacons Hill to the railway station.

JIM GILMORE
THE SWEEP 1940's

For many years Jim Gilmore the sweep was a familiar figure on the streets of Denbigh. He carried the tools of his trade on his bicycle and his services, particularly in pre-central heating days, were in great demand. It was with justifiable pride that he claimed not to leave a trace of soot behind after cleaning a chimney. Local onion growers were the grateful recipients of his bags of soot. Many Denbigh youngsters, eager to assist Jim Gilmore, were sent outside to patiently watch and signal the appearance of the brush from the chimney. In keeping with tradition, his son and grandson have followed the same line of business, albeit with more modern methods of operation.

HAROLD THE WATCH
1948

Harold Jones, or Harold the Watch as he was popularly known, was a native of Mold and it was his proud claim that as an infant, he sat on the lap of Daniel Owen (the eminent Welsh Novelist). He lived at 15, Bridge Street (now William Jones & Talog Davies, Solicitors) where he kept a jeweller's shop and his brother-in-law gave violin lessons. For years, Harold travelled the Denbigh district attending to grandfather and chapel clocks. He was a noted raconteur and his ready wit ensured his welcome into any company. He possessed a fine tenor voice and his knowledge of Welsh hymns was remarkable. A confirmed bachelor, but very much a ladies' man, he lived well into his nineties, leaving a well deserved reputation as a leading Denbigh character.